SPORTS STARTERS

Spike it Volleyball

John Crossingham

Crabtree Publishing Company

www.crabtreebooks.com

SPORTS STARTERS

Created by Bobbie Kalman

Dedicated by Katherine Kantor
To Father Bohdan Choly—thank you for all your inspiration and guidance.

Author
John Crossingham

Production coordinator
Katherine Kantor

Editors
Kelley MacAulay
Adrianna Morganelli
Robert Walker

Illustrations
Trevor Morgan: pages 4, 6, 8, 9, 10, 12, 14, 16, 18, 20, 22, 24, 26, 28, 30

Photo research
Crystal Sikkens

Photographs
All images by FIVB except:
© DPPI/Icon SMI: page 29
© 2008 Jupiterimages Corporation: page 17 (bottom)
© Photosport.com: page 18
© Shutterstock.com: pages 30, 31

Design
Margaret Amy Salter

Library and Archives Canada Cataloguing in Publication

Crossingham, John, 1974-
    Spike it volleyball / John Crossingham

(Sports starters)
Includes index.
ISBN 978-0-7787-3143-6 (bound).--ISBN 978-0-7787-3175-7 (pbk.)

    1. Volleyball--Juvenile literature. I. Title. II. Series: Sports
starters (St. Catharines, Ont.)

GV1015.34.C76 2008   j796.325   C2008-900930-4

Library of Congress Cataloging-in-Publication Data

Crossingham, John, 1974-
    Spike it volleyball / John Crossingham.
        p. cm. -- (Sports starters)
    Includes index.
    ISBN-13: 978-0-7787-3143-6 (rlb)
    ISBN-10: 0-7787-3143-X (rlb)
    ISBN-13: 978-0-7787-3175-7 (pb)
    ISBN-10: 0-7787-3175-8 (pb)
    1. Volleyball--Juvenile literature. I. Title.
    GV1015.34.C76 2008
    796.325--dc22

                                            2008004853

Crabtree Publishing Company

www.crabtreebooks.com   1-800-387-7650

Published in Canada
Crabtree Publishing
616 Welland Ave.
St. Catharines, Ontario
L2M 5V6

Published in the United States
Crabtree Publishing
PMB16A
350 Fifth Ave., Suite 3308
New York, NY 10118

Published in the United Kingdom
Crabtree Publishing
White Cross Mills
High Town, Lancaster
LA1 4XS

Published in Australia
Crabtree Publishing
386 Mt. Alexander Rd.
Ascot Vale (Melbourne)
VIC 3032

Contents

What is volleyball?

Volleyball is an indoor and outdoor team sport. A team sport is one that is played by groups of people against each other. Indoor volleyball is played on a wooden floor called a **court**. Outdoors, it is played on grass or sand. A game of volleyball is called a **match.**

*A volleyball team has six players on the court at a time. Any extra players are **substitutes**, or subs.*

Volleyball players are not allowed to hold or catch the ball.

Keep it up

Players bounce the ball over a net toward their opponents using their hands. Two teams hitting the ball back-and-forth to each other is called a **rally**. A team wins the rally by causing the other team to let the ball touch the floor. The team who wins the rally scores points.

Keeping score

A volleyball match has either three or five **sets**. To win matches, teams must win two out of three sets, or three of five sets. Teams get points by either having the ball land in their opponent's half of the court, or by having their opponents hit the ball out-of-bounds.

At the end of each set, teams switch the ends on which they are playing.

Win by two

Usually, the first team to score 15 points wins the set. But, teams must win a set by at least two points. So, if the teams are tied at 14, one team needs at least 16 points to win the set. Play continues until one team has two more points than the other.

Serve to score

Teams take turns **serving** the ball to each other. When one team is serving, the other team is receiving. Only the serving team can score points. If that team wins the rally, they get a point. If the receiving team wins the rally, they get a **side-out**. Now they serve and can try to score points.

In international volleyball, both the serving and receiving teams can score points. Each set goes to 25 points, except for the fifth set, which only goes to 15.

Court date

An indoor volleyball court is divided in half by a net. Each team plays on one side of the net. Each side has an **attack line**, which separates the **front court** and the **back court**.

free zone

Out of play

The area outside the court is called the **free zone**. A ball that lands here is out-of-bounds. When one team sends the ball into the free zone, that means a point for the opposition. The only time a player hits a ball from the free zone is when they are serving.

Volleyball players do not play the same position the whole match. They rotate positions often, from the front court to the back court.

Handling the ball

To play volleyball well, players use a few important moves, or actions. These pages show some of the most common volleyball moves.

*The **bump** (or pass) is used to handle an opponent's serve or **attack**. The ball is hit using the inside part of the joined forearms.*

*Volleying is done to set up a player to drive the ball into the **opposition's** court. To volley (or set) the ball, a player uses his or her fingertips to push the ball into the air.*

A **serve** begins the play in a volleyball match. A player on one team hits the ball in an overhand or underhand motion to the other team.

A **block** is used to stop a spike. One or more front court players leap at the net and raise their arms to stop the ball. A great block hits the ball right back at the spiker!

A leaping shot over the net is called a **spike**. To spike, a player jumps up and smashes the ball down with his hand.

A **dig** is a diving bump, used to get balls that are almost out of reach and close to the ground.

The front court

When volleyball players are in the front court they are mainly playing **offense**. Players who are playing offense are trying to score points. These players are volleying, leaping up, and spiking the ball into the opposition's court.

Players are very careful not to touch the net, which is against the rules.

Working together

A team can only touch the ball three times before hitting it back to the opposition. Teammates in the front court watch each other closely to set up attacks. They have to decide quickly who will volley the ball and who will spike it.

The player on the left has used a volley to set his front court teammate up for a strong spike.

The back court

Teammates in the back court are mainly playing **defense**. Players on defense are trying to get the ball up to the front court quickly to set up an attack. Defensive players often use moves like bumps and digs to move the ball forward.

Back court players wait crouched and ready for any balls that come their way.

Good positioning

Most of an opposing team's shots and serves land in the back court. Sometimes, the balls are moving very fast! Back court players use short, quick steps to get a good position under these shots. Once they are under the ball, back court players can bump it to the front court players.

Players in the back court often use a bump to set the ball up for players in the front court.

At your service

Every player must be able to serve—
it is one of the most important skills
in volleyball. The perfect serve is
hard and fast, but it also must land
inside the court. A serve that lands
in the free zone is a **fault**. A fault
gives the opposing team a side-out.

If a serve is not touched by an opposing player before it hits the ground,
*it is called an **ace**. An ace wins the serving team easy points!*

Over and under

Volleyballs can be served either overhand (top) or underhand (bottom). When serving overhand, the player tosses the ball into the air with one hand, hitting it with the other hand above shoulder-level. Overhand serves are fast and hard, and can be difficult to control. An underhand serve is hit at waist level. Players hold the ball with one hand, letting go as they hit it with the other hand. Underhand serves are easier to control, but are very slow moving.

overhand serve

underhand serve

17

Bump and volley

Bumping and volleying (setting) are important parts of playing offense. The bump is often the first contact a team makes with the ball. A bump slows the ball and allows players to get ready for an offensive attack.

A well-timed bump sets the front court players up for a strong offensive attack.

Set it up

The volley (set) is often the second hit a team makes with the ball. The goal of a volley is to put the ball high in the air and near the net, making it easy for teammates to spike it. Sometimes, a player will use a volley to put the ball into the opposing side's court (this is called a **dump**).

This volley was made high and close to the net, making it easier for teammates to spike.

Spike it!

The spike is usually the third contact a team makes with the ball. A player will leap into the air, striking the ball hard with one hand into the opposing side's court. The goal is to hit the ball hard enough so that the opposition can't return it.

Spikes require great timing. Players want to meet the ball at the highest point of their jump, making it difficult for the opposition to stop.

Run and jump

Players use a short, quick run-up to the ball when spiking. This run gives them more height in their jump. Some players like to start running from the free zone. This is called an **outside hit**. You can do this as long as the ball crosses the net between the **antennae**.

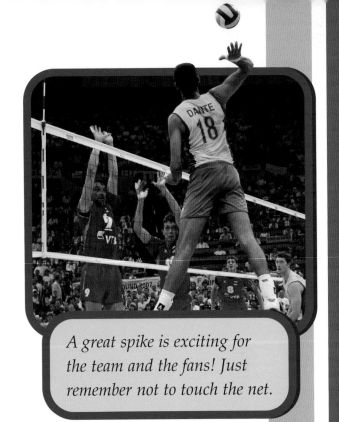

A great spike is exciting for the team and the fans! Just remember not to touch the net.

Tip you off

Sometimes, you can fool opponents by **tipping** the ball instead of spiking. A tip looks just like a spike, except instead of striking the ball, players gently nudge the ball over the net. This can catch defenders (who are expecting a hard hit) off-guard.

A gentle tip works best if the opposing blockers are lined up close to the net.

Block party

Blocking is an important front court defensive skill. Great blocks make it very difficult for opponents to shoot spikes over the net.

Often two or more players will get together to block a spike.

Watchful eyes

When the other team has the ball, players watch to see where their opponents might try to shoot the ball. If they see the ball being set up for a spike, front court players get ready to set up a block.

Up and away

When blocking, players stretch their arms to try to make themselves as tall as possible. Players do not hit the ball when they block. Instead, the ball just bounces off them and back over the net.

Blocking players cannot touch the net, but they may put their hands over the net if they can reach. Reaching over the net helps make sure the ball stays on the other side!

Rules and referees

Volleyball matches have **officials** who make sure that everyone plays by the rules. Top level matches have five officials who work together. A **referee** is the head official. A second referee, two **line judges,** and a scorekeeper are the other officials who help.

Referees use different hand signals to indicate plays made during the match.

Who's fault is it?

When a volleyball rule is broken, it is called a fault. When a fault occurs, a **penalty** is given. Some faults are common, such as touching the net, or a team hitting the ball more than three times in a row. For these faults, the penalty is either a point or a side-out for the other team.

The referee often uses yellow and red cards to announce penalties.

Hey, don't be rude!

Players should always show respect toward their opponents and officials. If players are rude toward anyone on the court, they can be sent off the court and miss a set. The worst offenders are disqualified and must leave the court for the whole match!

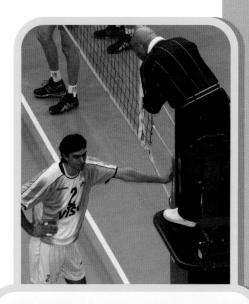

The referee deserves respect. Only the coach and team captain can question the referee about decisions.

At the beach

Aside from its sandy playing surface, **beach volleyball** is a lot like indoor volleyball. Many of the rules are the same, but in beach volleyball, teams are made up of two players instead of six.

A serious game

Don't let the swimsuits fool you—beach
volleyball is just as intense as when played
indoors. Teams compete at a professional
level across the world.

FIVB and the Olympics

There are many volleyball tournaments held around the world by **FIVB**. FIVB stands for Federation Internationale de Volleyball. The FIVB decides all of the rules and major competitions in the sport.

Russia, the U.S.A., Brazil, China, and Japan are some of the world's best volleyball nations.

For their country

The greatest honor for volleyball players is to be part of their country's national team. Athletes play for their countries at many international tournaments, including the **Olympics** and the **World Cup.**

Only the greatest

National teams play all year for the right to compete in these top tournaments. Only 12 teams play men's and women's Olympic volleyball. These teams train hard even though they make very little money from their sport.

Brazil's Emanuel Rego (left) and Ricardo Santos celebrate after winning the gold medal match against Spain in the men's beach volleyball competition at the Athens 2004 Olympic Games.

Have a ball

Volleyball is an excellent sport for kids. It builds teamwork and can be played indoors or outside. Chances are, there's a volleyball team in your area that you can join.

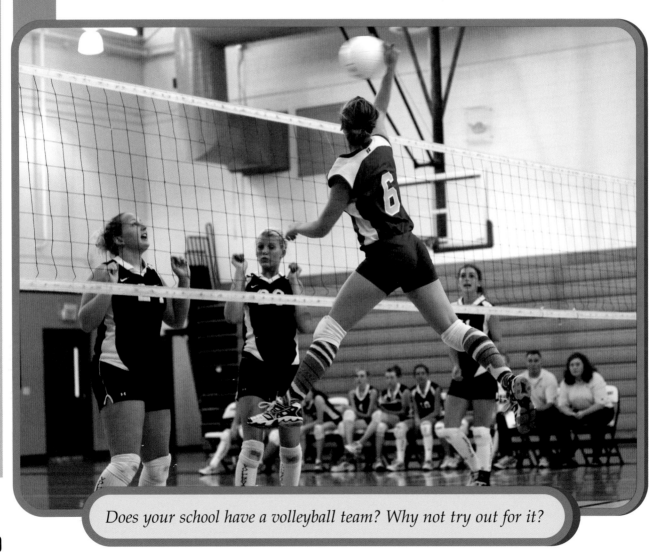

Does your school have a volleyball team? Why not try out for it?

Beach party

Local beach volleyball leagues are also a great start. Many beaches or sports clubs have summer leagues for many age groups.

On your own

If you find leagues a bit scary, don't worry. You can just play a simple game of volleyball with a few friends. Just grab a net, a ball, and an open space, and get started. Have fun!

Don't forget your sunblock when playing volleyball at the beach!

Glossary

Note: Some boldfaced words are defined where they appear in the book.

ace A serve that lands within the lines without being touched by the other team

antennae The flexible, vertical rods at the ends of a volleyball net

attack Players working to score a point against opponents

back court The area between the attack line and the end line

court The surface where a volleyball game is played, featuring a net and line markings

opposition Players on the other team

fault An illegal move or play

free zone The area outside the side and end lines of the court (out-of-bounds)

front court The area between the attack line and the net

line judge An official who identifies balls that are hit out-of-bounds

match A competition consisting of three or five games

Olympics A modern multi-sport competition held every four years with teams from across the world

penalty A punishment for a fault

serving A player strikes the ball into the opposition's court, beginning play

set The scoring design of a volleyball game

side-out The transfer of service from one team to another after the serving team loses a rally

substitute An extra player who waits on the bench to play; also called a sub

World Cup A competition for both men and women, qualifying teams for the Olympics

Index

Printed in the U.S.A.